What Can Go?

by Ellen Dalton • illustrated by Kyle Poling

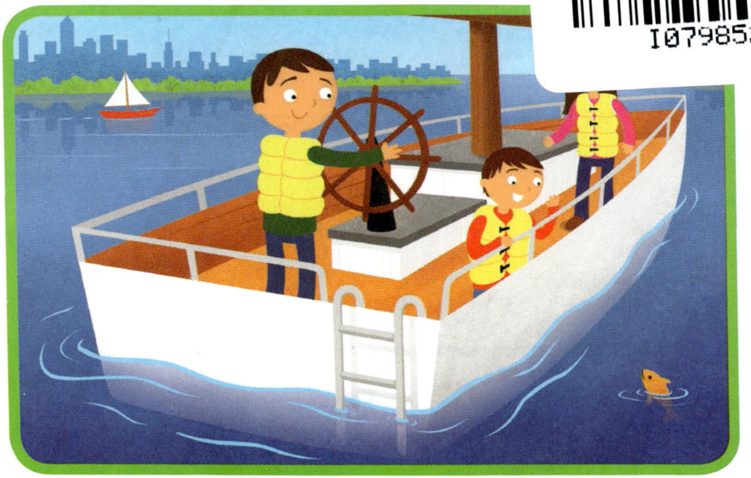

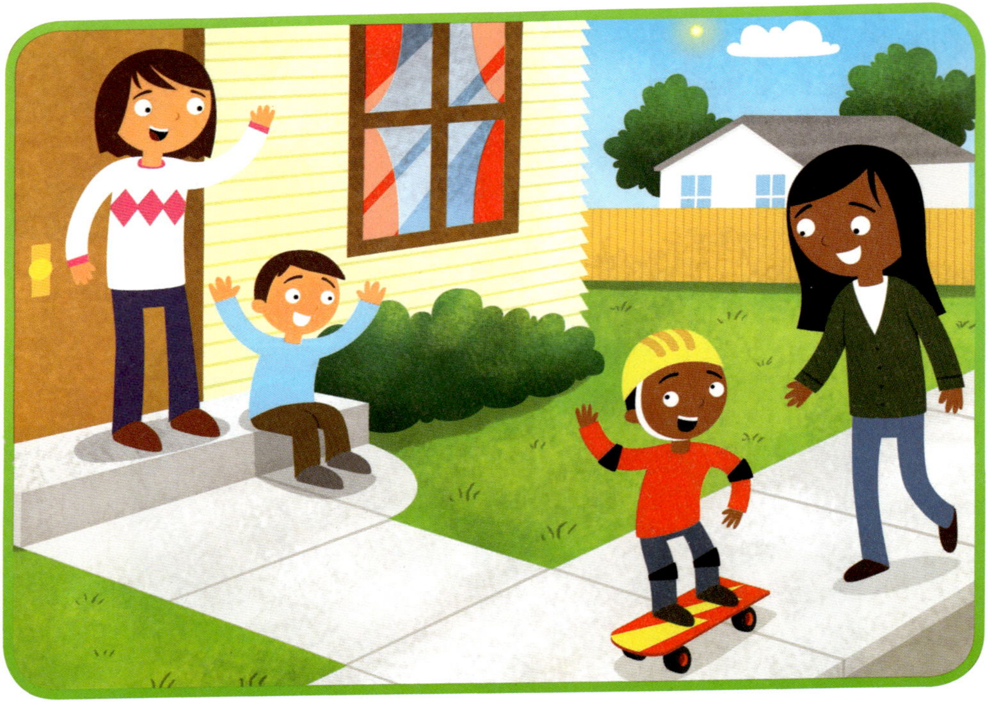

A 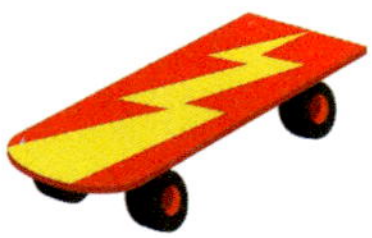 skateboard can go.

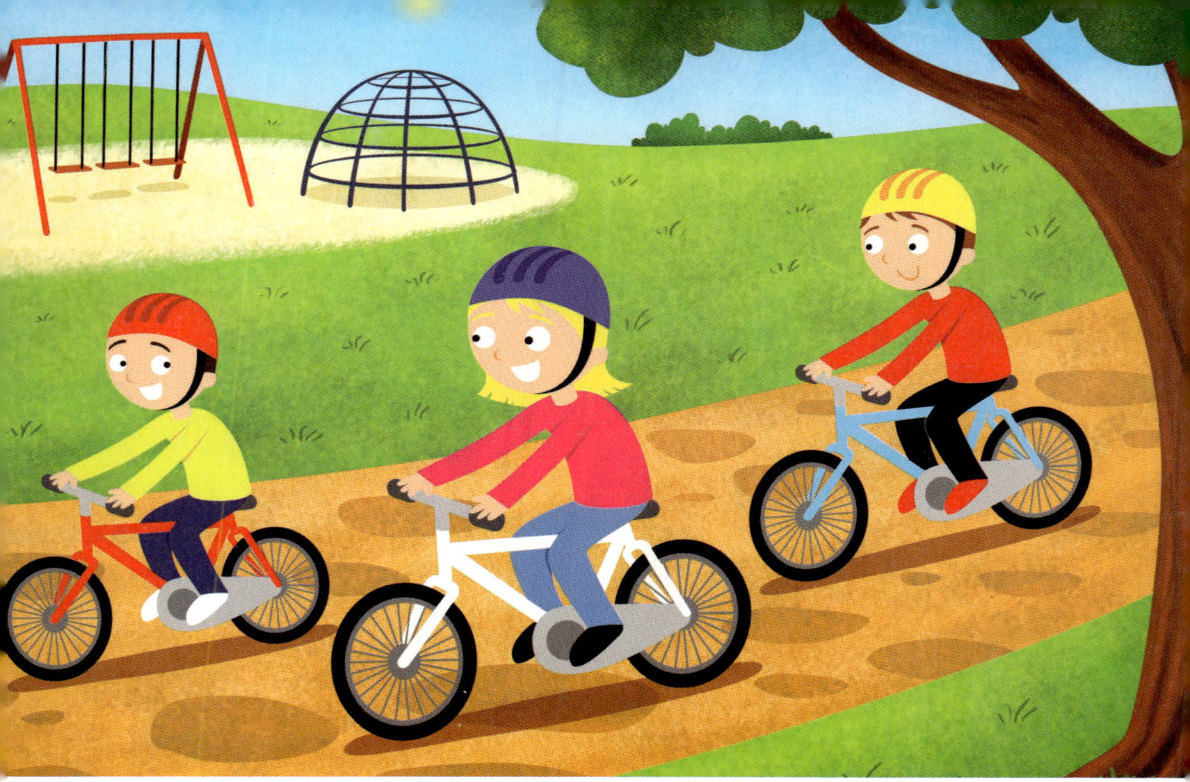

A 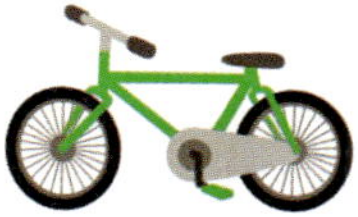 can go.

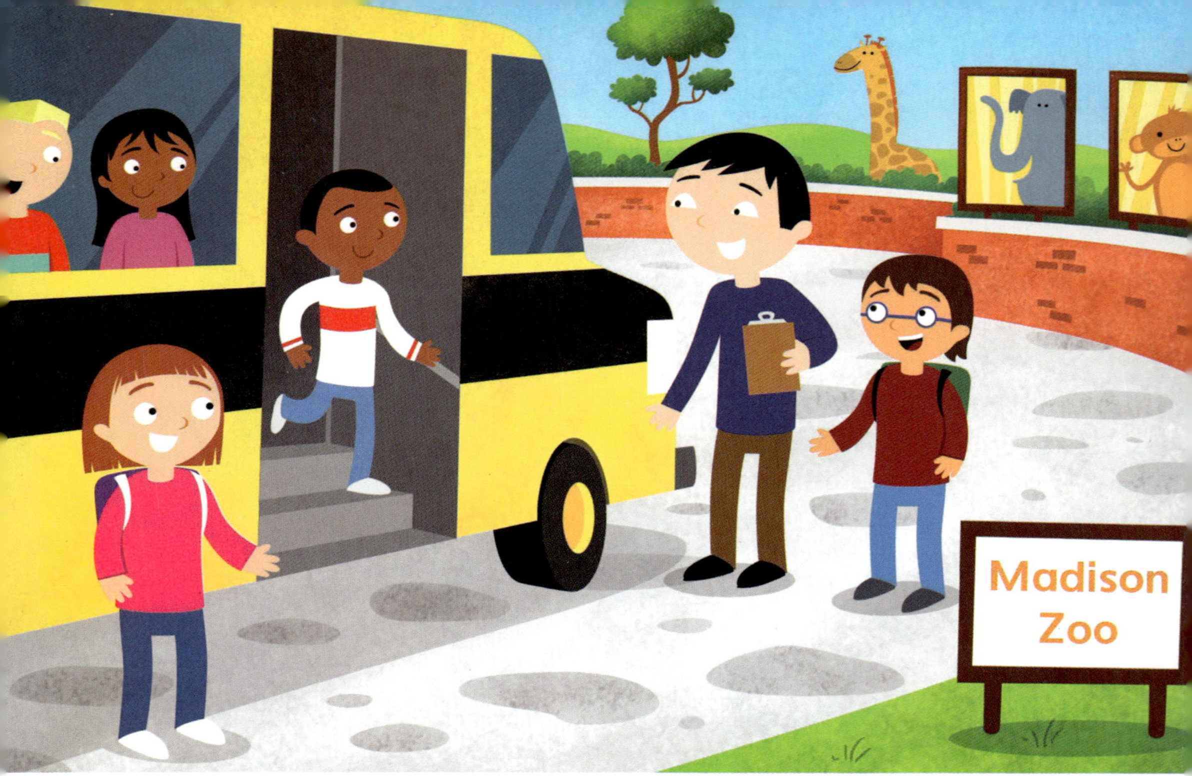

A 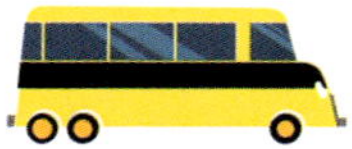 bus can go.

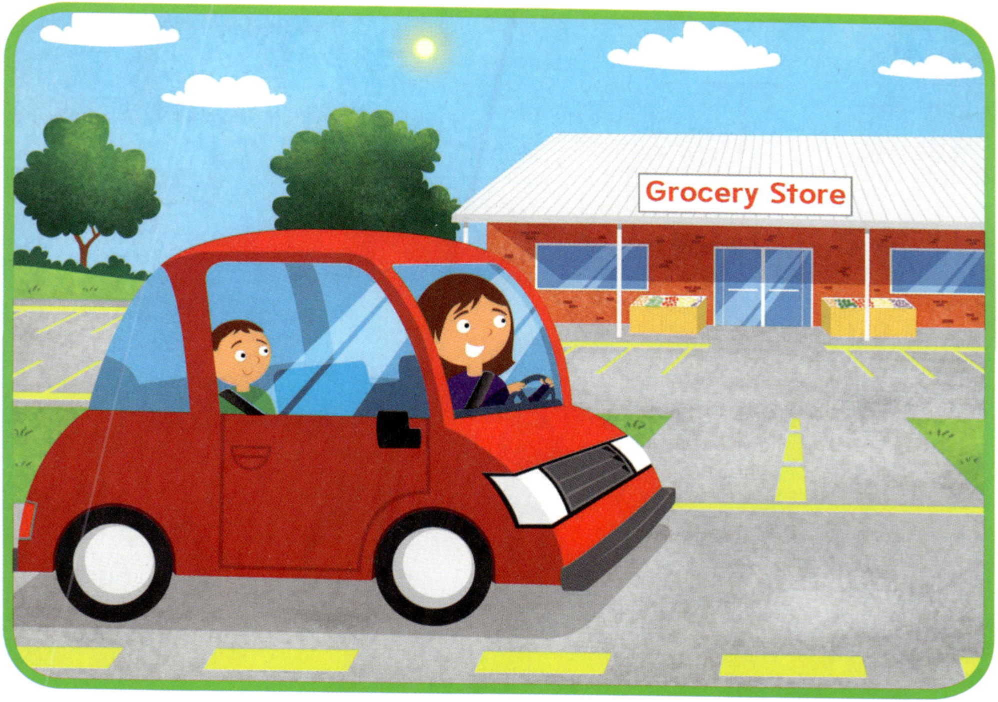

A 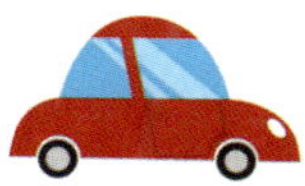 car can go.

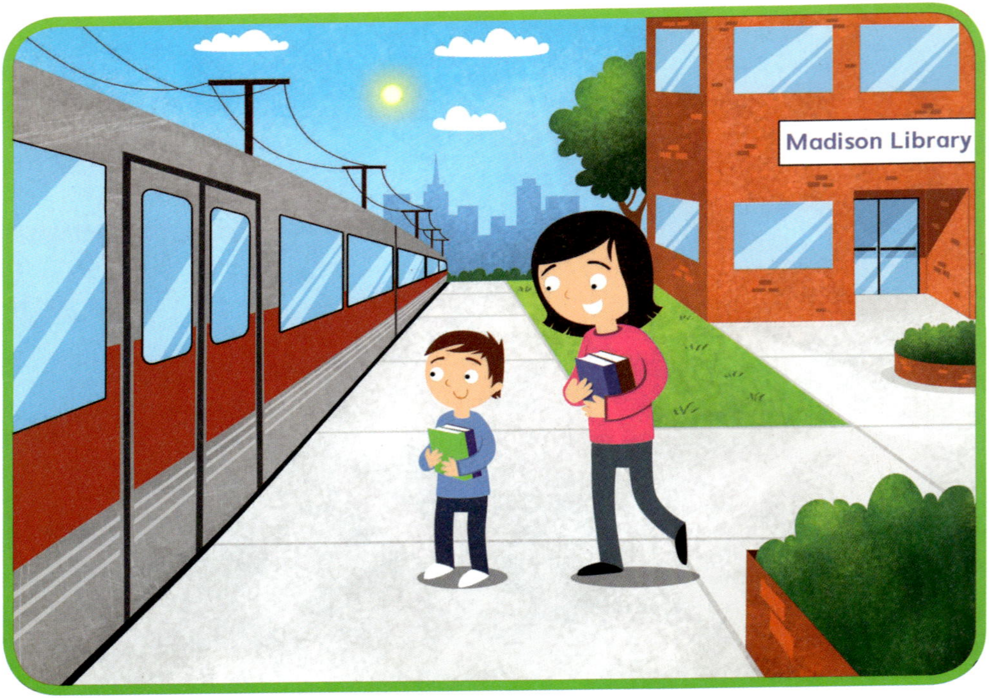

A 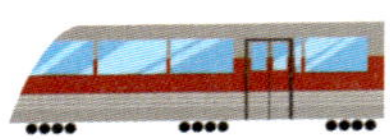 train can go.

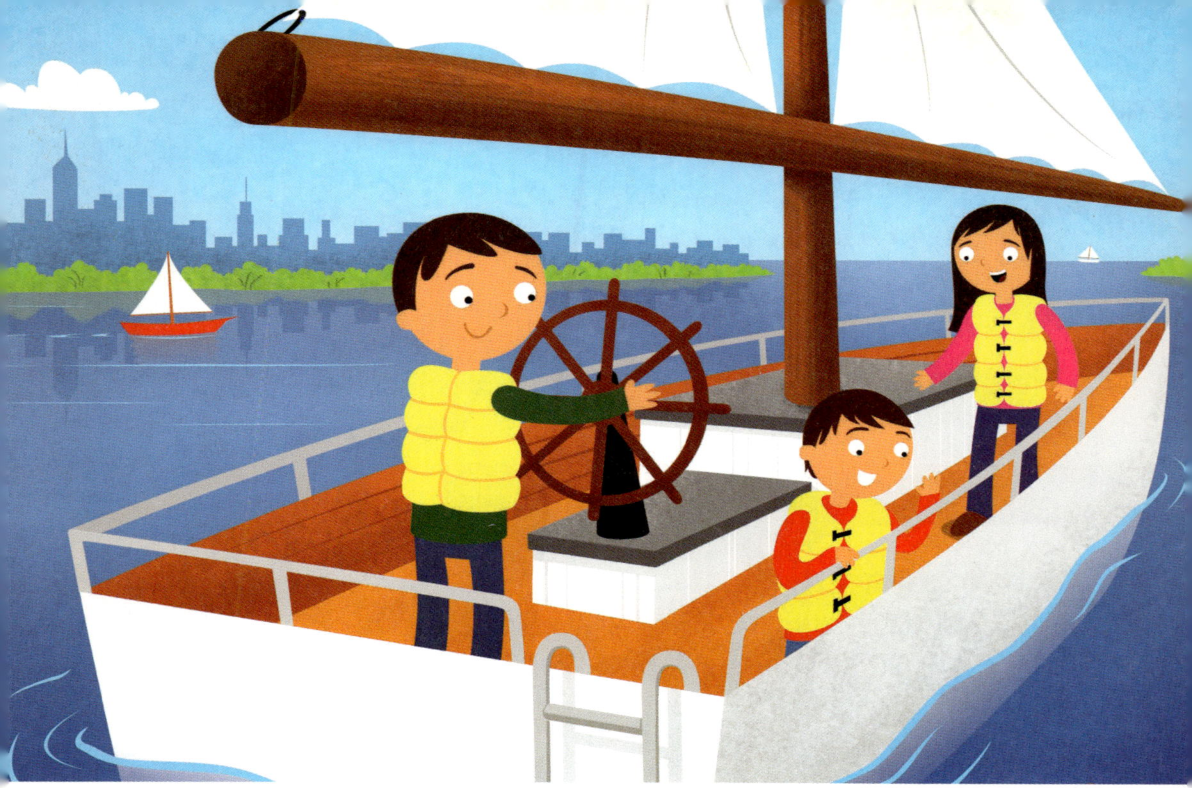

A 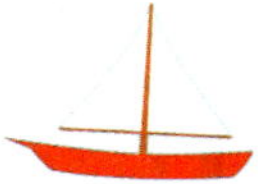 boat can go.

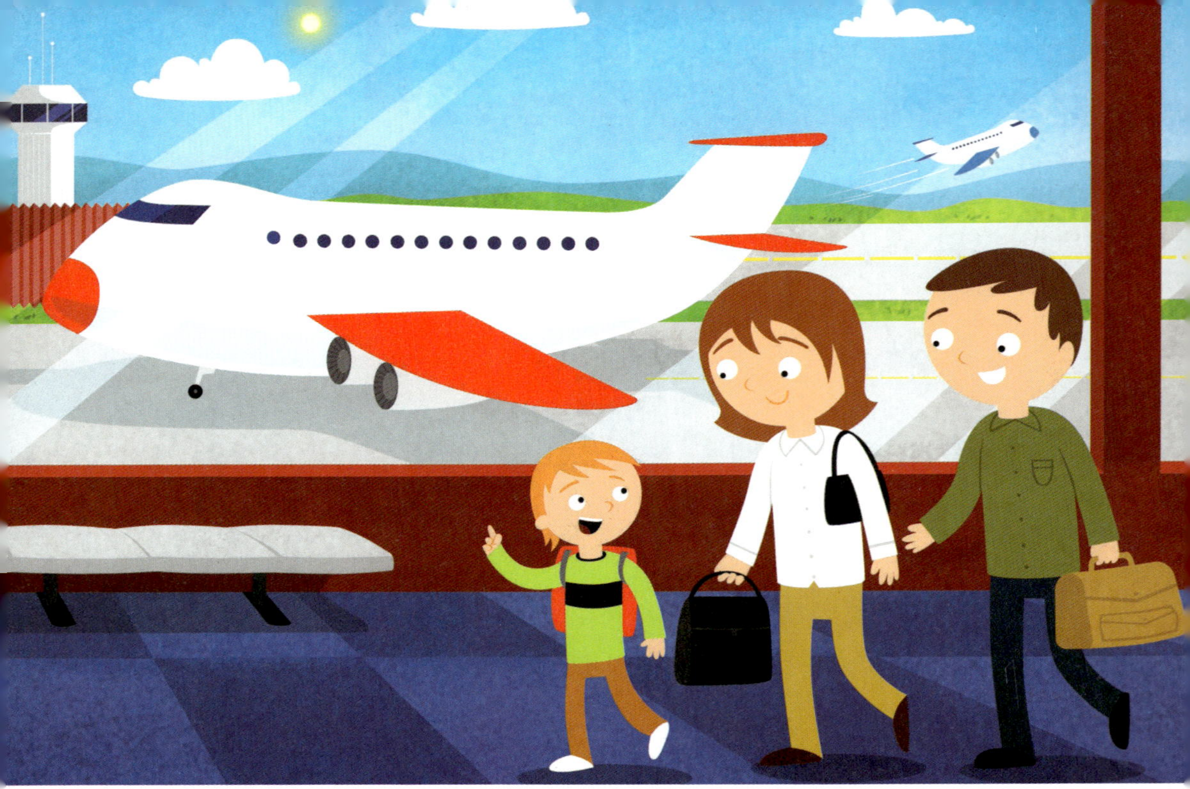

A kid can go!